Donna Leon

Gondola

With a CD of Venetian barcarole *performed by Il Pomo d'Oro,*

conducted by Riccardo Minasi,

featuring Vincenzo Capezzuto and Cecilia Bartoli

D0037545

Atlantic Monthly Press
New York

For Christine Stemmermann

With thanks to Shaul Bassi and Philip Morre for their assistance with the barcarole translations

Published simultaneously in Canada
Printed in the United States of America

FIRST EDITION

ISBN 978-0-8021-2266-7
eISBN 978-0-8021-9252-3

Atlantic Monthly Press
an imprint of Grove Atlantic, Inc.
154 West 14th Street
New York, NY 10011

Distributed by Publishers Group West
www.groveatlantic.com
14 15 16 17 10 9 8 7 6 5 4 3 2 1

Contents

Introduction

That Venice is in peril is a fact so universally acknowledged that one of the committees which raises funds to aid in the restoration of works of art in the city bears that name: *Venice in Peril*. It is in peril from climate change, declining population, mass tourism, cruise ships, and from the various agencies of government which seem deaf to the voices of its citizens. At the same time, however, attempts are being made to control the effect of the tides and to prevent the assault of *acqua alta,* Teatro La Fenice has been rebuilt, and there is always the compensation of the beauty which surrounds residents or tourists anywhere in the city.

Part of that beauty on common offer is the sleek, mysterious gondola, the boat whose name and image are inextricably linked with the city. For centuries its blade-like hull has been cutting through the waters of the canals, taking people to and from home, the Rialto, assignations, work. Rowing from the back is the *gondoliere*, once the trusted servant, sometimes confidant, of families, today but another worker in the tourist industry.

Just as the gondola has remained recognizably the same through the centuries, so too have the *barcarole* which were

sung from their decks centuries ago. Like the boat, these songs are quintessentially Venetian: sung in dialect, they present the real life and concerns of the people in the city. Venice once created a mercantile empire, and sacked Byzantium, but its citizens worried about love. The city itself ultimately fell to the invasion of Napoleon, but the Venetians went on drinking too much and longing after girls. Their hopes and desires fill the lyrics of the barcarole, and the music – at times sophisticated, at times simple – carries the listener along the tides of beauty just as does the gondola, from whose decks these lovely songs were first heard.

The Gondola as a Paradox

The stunned response of many people who come to Venice for the first time is to gasp in amazement at the glory of what they see. Magnificent buildings line up in chronological disarray; neighborhoods are connected to one another only by bridges; the Basilica of San Marco appears drunk on domes and gold, and most streets seem undecided about where they are going.

A suitable response to the city would be to laugh in amazement at the things that, by rights, should not be. Those buildings jostling one another are built on mud and water, aren't they? The historical and religious symbol of the city is a lion with wings, an aerodynamic and ornithological impossibility. Equally unlikely is the boat that is a palpable symbol of the city – the gondola – for it is, in open defiance of all shipbuilding logic, asymmetrical, longer on the right side. It is flat-bottomed and propelled by a standing man rowing from one side with a single oar. Further, in today's speed-obsessed world, this boat lacks a motor, generally moves at the pace of a walking man, and is no longer subjected to frequent design alterations to increase its speed or maneuverability.

This hardly sounds like a combination that is going to meet with great success, yet Venice was, for centuries, the center of the Western World in terms of wealth, luxury, and military might. Those apparently floating buildings were, in reality, firmly based on wealth and political stability. The lion was no docile tabby: the armies of Venice stormed the walls of Byzantium and conquered an empire, then sacked it and brought the booty home, where the gondola moved people and goods through the city quickly and easily. All three might have looked strange, but by heaven, they achieved all of this.

Once the most important city in the West, Venice is today a tiny provincial town of fewer than 60,000 residents. It can, however, be argued that it is the most beautiful city in the world as well as the best known. It's been there more than a thousand years. The buildings have been redesigned, stripped bare, reconstructed, flooded and burned. History has clipped the lion's wings as the city fell victim to the invading armies of the French, the Austrians, the Germans, and now the tourists. The gondola, too, has undergone countless changes in the centuries that gondolieri have been rowing it silently through the canals; the prow has gained height, and the boat has been made flatter and wider, then changed shape to its modern appearance. It was stripped bare of decoration and forced by law to be black. Yet it remains as unmistakable a symbol of a city as the Parthenon, the Coliseum, the World Trade Center. Those others are in ruins, or gone, but the gondola is still going about its quiet business of taking people from one place in the city to another. Ten centuries have passed, and it's still made by specialist artisans of the same types of wood; prow and stern are still protected by ornamented metal strips; and its gondoliere still moves it at an amble through the waterways of Venice.

Much about the city can be learned by a close look at the gondola, its construction and history, its place in the culture, the fascination with which it is viewed by Venetians and non-Venetians alike. *La gondola* is the longest-lived female in the city and the most fascinating. Like the pasts of many beautiful women, hers is clothed in mystery, and the stories told about her often conflict with one another. Her appearance has changed over the years; many men have adored her: Goethe, Rousseau, Chateaubriand. Though not a widow, she always wears black. Though of uncertain origins her true name can be pronounced only in Veneziano. "*Gondola*," when pronounced in Italian, sounds almost right, but not quite, for there should be no "l" in her name when it is said in her native dialect. Thus, no matter how often – like her home city – she is at the service of foreigners, she is destined to remain forever and completely Venexiana, as are the barcarole that accompany this book.

By taking a look at the gondola and the vital role she played in the founding of Venice, and hearing the music performed on her deck, one can perhaps enter into the life of the city in a new way: from the water, from the back doors, that part of the city familiar to those who know and love her best. It's a different point of view and, unlike much of the city today, entirely Venetian.

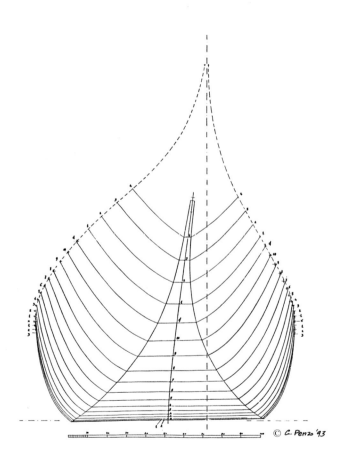

© C. Penzo '93

I Think I Could Do This

B ecause gondolas, to any of us who have lived in Venice for decades, are as common as yellow taxis to a New Yorker, we almost cease to notice them, and thus we seldom give them conscious thought. We passively observe that all other boats defer to them and give them right of way, and the shout of the gondolieri approaching a turn is part of the background noise of the city. If we use them at all, it is as a convenient *traghetto* service to cross the Grand Canal when we are in a hurry or burdened with produce from the Rialto Market. Thus it was only by force of coincidence that they their familiar invisibility entered my conscious mind, aroused my curiosity and, after some time, led to this book and disc.

About nine years ago, an American friend was given as a Christmas present – I believe it was meant to be a joke – the blueprints of a gondola, complete with detailed instructions. He opened the plans and began to spread them out on the dinner table. As he unfolded the paper, more and more bottles, plates, and cutlery had to be removed to the sideboard or taken back into the kitchen. The paper expanded. When the sides of the blueprint were hanging over the four sides of the table, he turned from them and began to read the instructions that accompanied them.

The other guests at the dinner were forced to balance their plates on their knees or abandon the idea of food altogether and content themselves with wine and conversation. If it is possible to ignore a person looming over a two-meter long blueprint, muttering to himself, then we ignored him. Until suddenly he said, his face alight with a vision of the finished gondola, "I think I could do this."

The other revelation also came at dinner, as is so often the case in Italy, though this was in a different part of the city and with different guests. A friend lives on the Grand Canal, which means glory and beauty and bliss and endless delight. It also means, alas, gondola-loads of tourists back and forth under the windows, and since these are the gondolas working with large groups of tourists, an accordionist and a singer are tossed in. (Oh, how tempting is that phrase.)

As we ate our risotto, we heard the – dare I use this word? – music approaching. The accordionist squeezed out some notes, and the voice of what I had once heard my Irish grandmother call "a whisky tenor" rose up to the mezzanine apartment, and the words of "O sole mio," flew up to scandalize us all.

At that point, the host's dachshund, Artù, leaped up (well, he struggled up because he was a dachshund) onto the wide windowsill, pitched his head back, and began to howl like what that same grandmother would call a banshee. Beside himself, either with the pain caused by the music – pain which we shared – or perhaps deluding himself that this noise came from his dog pack and he was being called upon to declare his solidarity with them, Artù howled his head off whilst the boatloads of tourists below snapped photographs and waved up at him. During this, the gondolier, not the tenor, shouted up, "*Ciao, Artù. Che togo che ti xe.*" I have many friends who are singers: none of them has ever had a gondoliere call up to tell him what a wonderful singer he is, nor has any one of them been photographed, head back and howling, by boatloads of Japanese tourists.

Let me leave Artù to his art and return my attention to the Master Builder. Construction began, not in Venice but about an hour from the city, where my American friend had access to a complete carpenter's workshop with ample space to work

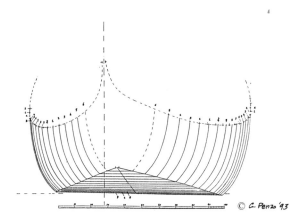

© C. Penzo '93

on the boat. No, he is not a professional carpenter, though he has for years built cabinets, tables, doors, even an elaborate drop-front writing desk. But not, until then, had he thought of building a gondola. Alone.

A year passed. Every so often, I went to visit him and to have a look at the project, feeling not a little like Catherine the Great stopping by to see how the Hermitage was progressing. I spent the good part of one afternoon watching him curve the oak boards that would form the sides of the gondola. This required that they be kept wet on the top while he played a blowtorch across them from below as-he molded the eleven-meter planks into the proper shape. The frame took a year, and then he began to insert the *sancón* and the *piàna*, the stabilizing bars that run from side to side of the bottom and would eventually be covered by the floorboards or *pagiòl*. I realized how much an exercise in three-dimensionality the construction was, for the two sides curve up – as if the boat were a giant lopsided banana – to encompass a hollow space, and the builder must continually calculate just what is next and where it is going to go in relation to the other pieces.

As another year passed, the area covered by his project expanded, until one room of the carpenter's workshop was filled with lengths of wood, rectangles of wood, rods and strips and pegs and pieces for which there is no English – and no Italian – name. Not only had a large section of the workshop been turned into *uno squero*, but one of his workbenches was

now home to scores of oddly-shaped pieces of wood. Stranger still, the Italian carpenter often asked the American to explain to him the details of cutting and planing the *nómbolo* (side planks), *pirón* (wooden bolts and nails), and *pontapìe* (inclined wooden brace for the gondoliere's back foot). As to the *trèsso*, the carpenter's uncertainty might result from this definition given it: "listelli fissati sull'orlo interno di alcuni *sancóni* per sostenere rispettivamente il *sentàr*, le banchéte e il *tristolìn* da *próva* inferiore". Obviously, these are instructions that make sense only to a Venetian gondola builder. Eventually, the carpenter was to observe the creation of more than two hundred structural and semi-structural, functional and non-functional parts, including a large number of simple wooden planks. Here I should add that the gondola, unlike the jigsaw puzzle, does not come with ready-cut pieces. The person − though it is virtually unheard of that a single person should attempt it − who builds the boat has to cut each piece by hand or machine and shape it so precisely that it fits smoothly into the pieces around it. Water-tight, remember?

Another year passed, and my friend arrived at the *trasto de mèso* and began thinking about where to find the most beautiful *fórcola*, upon which the oar is braced, though I had learned enough by then to realize there was going to be no need of a fórcola for some time yet, at least a year. The fórcola can't be slipped into place until the entire boat is completed, but I chose to interpret his interest as optimism, not magical thinking. As the boat grew, the room began to clear: less space was taken up by unused pieces, just as the closer one comes to completing a puzzle, the fewer pieces lie loose on the table.

Towards the beginning of the fourth year, he reached the point of constructing the *parti decorative*, the *sentolìna* and the *caenèla*. By then, the carpenter had been transformed from a rent-collecting Saul to a Saint Paul, fully converted and eager to participate, although my friend allowed him to help only with heavy lifting, never with the actual work of construction.

When the frame was complete, it was necessary to caulk, which is done with thin strings of cotton that must be soaked in resin and then wedged into the tiny grooves between the interlocking boards from which the boat is built. These strings are sealed in place with repeated coats of resin; later, before it's painted, pitch will be used to seal the complete interior of the gondola.

While he's busy sealing up the boat to make sure it's watertight, let's go back to Artù, the Fritz Wunderlich of Palazzo Curti Valmarana. Through the days and evenings of a hot summer, the tourists floated by, the accordionist played, and Artù conquered. An American movie producer, hearing Artù in concert, talked of the possibility of his appearing in a cameo role in a new film version of *Romeo e Giulietta*. Even though we knew that the words of American film producers are as permanent as what is written on the waters of the Grand Canal, a few of us permitted ourselves an evening discussing

costumes and shooting angles. I remember one heated discussion of whether Artù's right profile was better than his left and from which side, therefore, to film him. I'm afraid I grew quite severe here and suggested that, should negotiations ever lead to this point, the only place from which to shoot Artù was the floor.

Time passed, and his owner did not hear from the producer, and finally the film was made without Artù's artistic contribution. He, however, continued to sing. As the months went by and I heard the repertory of the human singers time after time, I realized that the two most often-sung songs that waft their way up and down the waters of the Grand Canal are those Neapolitan classics, "*Torna a Sorrento*" and "*O sole mio.*" Was a Venetian dog meant to sing along to these? What, I wondered, was the music that was really meant to be sung from the gondola?

By the middle of the fifth year, the gondola was caulked, coated with countless layers of resin, painted, and judged to be watertight. All of the decorative parts were in place, the fórcola bought, and two metal *ferri* attached at front and back. It was time to launch the gondola. To do this, it was necessary to find enough strong men to take it from where it rested in the wooden cradle in the carpenter's workshop and carry it first to a truck. Thirty-two men answered the casting call, a panoply of muscles such as life seldom presents us. They lifted the gondola, all 350 kilos of it, and carried it slowly towards an eight-wheeled heavy transport truck. The driver lowered the winch and then lifted the boat into place on the cradle where it would rest until it reached its destination.

The trip took an hour. I followed behind in a friend's car and thus could see the heads of drivers and passengers whip around as the truck passed them. A gondola? On the *autostrada*?

In Tronchetto, the parking lot at the end of the bridge from the mainland, another winch cradled the gondola and lifted it from the truck, then lowered it gently into the water. As soon as they heard the story, the people in the growing crowd at the dock, lined up on the edge, waiting to see if it would sink or swim.

It swam, and the heroic builder finally climbed down into his boat, walked to the back, and took the oar that a friend handed down to him. In jeans and tennis shoes, without a straw hat, and with no Neapolitan singer at midship, he started to row away from the dock, heading towards the entrance to the Grand Canal.

Those of us who had come along with him to Venice to watch the launch started to cheer, and soon we were joined by the workers on the pier. Our shouts and whistles must have created a strong wind or current behind him, for very soon he disappeared into the darkness under the railway bridge. Then, a few long minutes later, he appeared again in the sunlight on the other side, turned in an arc to the right, and disappeared into the beginning of the Grand Canal. This time, it was the assembled dock workers and boatmen who started to cheer, and soon we were all standing there, pounding one another on the shoulder, cheering at the boat that was finally on its way towards home.

Taking a Closer Look

Despite some changes in its form, the gondola we see today, gliding effortlessly through the waters of Venice, is easily recognizable as the same boat that floats through the work of the great painters of Venice: Bellini, Canaletto, Carpaccio, Guardi. To walk through any museum where their paintings or drawings are on display is to identify, not only the gondola, but the familiar buildings and bridges of the city, just as faces identical to many of the subjects in those paintings can today appear behind the counter of a bar or across a Venetian dinner table. Part of the fascination of the city surely rests in the fact that the past is so ever-present genetically as well as linguistically and architecturally.

Though there is speculation, though no certainty, about the origins of this very strange boat, today it is seen as the quintessential Venetian. Its name has changed, though there is philological dispute about the nature of that change. Some insist that the original name came from Greek, "*kóndy*" (cup). Or perhaps the origin is the Latin "*concula*" (small shell) or "cymbula" (little boat). The first written evidence of the current name comes from a 1094 decree by Doge Vitale Falier, making mention of the "*Gondulam*".

The symbiotic relationship, if that's what it is, between Venice and the gondola puts one in mind of the chicken-egg dilemma. Which came first, an exquisitely maneuverable, light boat that a single man could propel effortlessly through shallow, reed-lined canals and so save the population of the Veneto from the hordes of invaders from the North? Or was it the growing need to flee into the marshy land off the coast of what is today Venice that required the construction of a boat that could carry people to safety? Bear in mind, as well, the tremendous advantage had by a rower who is looking forward as the boat moves and is thus able to see what dangers lie ahead. A change in tide, unexpected by the invaders in their deep-keeled boats, who were unfamiliar with channels and tidal patterns, would ground them in the mud of receding waters, leaving them easy targets for the Venetians, intimately familiar with every curve their canals made through the marshes. The gondola is not likely to be confused with a man-of-war, but there can be no question of its tactical superiority in the marshy terrain that is its home territory.

By the early part of the Sixteenth Century, Venice no longer at risk of invasion, the name "gondola" was in common usage, as was the boat, though this one was symmetrical and rowed by two rowers, one on either side. What distinguished it from other boats of similar lineaments was the use to which it was put. The others, even those rowed by men in the standing position, transported heavy loads of products and produce

meant to be sold and were used primarily for commercial purposes. At that time, the gondola was used almost exclusively for the private transport of persons of a certain rank. This fact would certainly help explain why it was the gondola upon which Venetian craftsmen lavished their attentions, in hopes of making it ever more beautiful, ever more eye-catching, ever more sellable. In our times, stuffed teddy bears are occasionally tied onto the front of sixteen-wheeled trucks, but it is the ornamentation of the Maserati that causes heads to turn.

Today's gondola, the one in which tourists are given their view of the back canals of the city, dates from the Nineteenth Century, when the boat builders Casal and Tramontin began to build the slimmer, asymmetrical gondolas we nowadays know. It is an elaborate construction, sometimes taking a squad of specialized workers as long as two years to complete. Its wooden pieces are still made of the same eight types of wood: fir, larch, oak, elm, cherry, mahogany, lime, and walnut. Almost 11 meters long, its flat bottom reduces the resistance to the water and renders it both fast and agile, as can be seen any year during the *regatta,* when both professional and amateur gondolieri display the remarkable skill with which they make these wooden boats move and turn.

It is said that a fully-laden gondola, loaded with passengers to a total weight of 700 kilos, can still move at the rate of a walking man. Further, the gondoliere who is rowing that mass exerts no more energy than if he were walking at a normal pace.

Reggatta Delle Donne

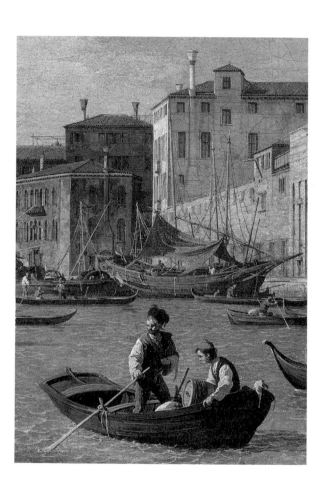

Both residents and tourists make frequent, quotidian use of those workhorse gondolas, or traghetti, which take people from one side to the other of the Grand Canal. They are to be found at Rialto (though this one finishes running at lunchtime) at Santa Fosca, San Tomà, and in front of the Hotel Gritti. These gondole have two oarsmen who effortlessly take twelve or more standing passengers across the canal for a mere seventy cents each. Tourists and non-residents have recently been zapped and must now pay two Euros to cross the Canal, while residents still pay the lower resident price. Considering the glory available on both sides of the Canal, and no matter which fare is paid, this ride might well be the greatest tourist bargain in the world.

The gondola's perfection lies in seeming imperfection. The boards making up the left side are longer, thus curving the asymetrical prow to the right. This would, obviously, render an ordinary boat unmaneuverable and condemn it to endless circles, no matter how carefully its two ordinary rowers worked. The force propelling the gondola, however, comes from only the right side and thus the disproportion works to the advantage of the single rower at the stern as he thrusts his weight forward to dig his oar into the water. At the end of his stroke, he slides the oar from the water, shifts his weight while bringing the oar forward, suspends it what seems only a millimeter above the water, only to slip it in again and continue his journey.

Though the gondolieri wore elaborate costumes in former times, created by specialized tailors, hat- and shoemakers, today their attire is reduced to an optional straw boater with a red ribbon and a black and white striped shirt, but there is no standard uniform. The trousers are usually black, though white Nike tennis shoes often peek out from beneath them. The only constant in appearance is the gondola itself, which is always black. There are many romantic (is "invented" the better word?) stories to explain this. There is the legend that the gondola wears black for those who died in the plague, or to mourn the city's conquest by Napoleon (though they were black centuries before that.) There exist records of sumptuary laws passed concerning the gondola – an attempt on the part of the city to keep its citizens from wasting their money in the attempt to outdo one another with ever more elaborate and ever more expensive decoration for their boats. So far as I have been able to learn, these laws were concerned more with excessive decoration than with color.

The gondola is made waterproof by being caulked and painted inside with pitch, and then many coats of resin are put on the outer shell before it is all covered in black paint. Always black nowadays, never white, say, or grey. Or yellow. Or even gold, as the ambassadorial gondolas – diplomats being exempt from the sumptuary laws – painted by Marieschi approximately in 1735, blindingly bright, looking as though it had been minted rather than built.

The choice of black might be explained by practicality, no surprise from a people as practical as the Venetians. Consider for a moment the perils presented by the geography of the city; think of water traffic, and waves, and drunken boatmen, and amateurs out for their first try at rowing, and narrow *canali* and sudden turns. And rough stone walls. Any one of these elements can lead to collision or scraping, as they still often do. What happens to the long black streak on the yellow – or white – hull, after the other guy has rowed beyond sight or hailing? What if the gondola is moored behind the *palazzo*, and a freak wind bangs it against the stone wall one night? How much easier to cover the scrapes by slapping on a few layers of black paint rather than try to match the original color. I am not certain that this is the reason the gondola is black, but it is a possibility and certainly makes as much sense as a vow made by gondolieri to thank God for saving the city from the plague. Or Napoleon.

Another way the gondola has changed – and the paintings of the Venetian school give endless evidence of its previous ubiquity as part of the gondola – is in the removal of the central cabin, the *felze.* The origin of its name, like that of the gondola, is disputed: the usual suspect is the Greek *phýlakos,* or protection, but no certain source can be found. Originally intended to protect passengers from the elements, it was made of thin cloth attached to a frame of wooden rods arching from one side of the gondola to the other, left open in front and back. Giovanni Mansueti's beautiful "Miraculous Healing of the Daughter of Benvegnudo" in the Gallerie dell'Accademia catches a brightly-dressed gondolier in the act of assembling the felze, its cloth as bright and patterned as those of his jacket and stockings. The lightness of fabric and construction suggest that the entire construction could easily be disassembled and removed from the gondola.

A hundred years later, most felzi had become as black as the gondola, and with the passage of another century, they became a permanent and unremovable wooden element in the gondola, now with thicker cloth as lining and curtains. Open windows on the sides, as well as the openings at front and back, allowed for greater visibility from inside as well as for the passage of more air through the enclosed space during the hot months. One has but to think of the smoke-glassed limousines and SUV's which often cruise by in the fast lane to get an idea of the effect: there was no way to see inside, though the passengers were free to view what was going on around them, if only by pulling back the curtain a few centimeters. Or, in the nineteenth century, by peering through one of the cracks in the wooden shutters that covered the side windows and the doors to the front and back openings, shutters which are now called, at least in English, Venetian blinds.

Pause and consider for a moment this situation: the man or woman of a noble house is enclosed and invisible inside the cloth or wood of the felze, so thick as to protect him or her from

the sun or wind, cold or damp. But think, if you will, from what else might the virtual invisibility provided by the *felze* protect a person. The eyes of neighbors? Friends? Wives? Husbands?

Rowing at the stern was the gondoliere, the only servant who who was treated with easy familiarity by his masters. He was young, tall, gaily dressed, strongly muscled. It is said and often written that the gondolier knew the family secrets and the intimate details of the private behavior of both husband and wife. Many stories are told of how attractive gondolieri often were, both to men and to women. The gondola – which was a house without being a house – was considered as *"un luogo d'incontor"* (a place for meeting) and the one person who would always know what went on during those encounters was the gondoliere. Or perhaps he played a part in them?

But let us leave such base thoughts behind and move to the essential decorative element of the gondola, *i ferri*, the metal ornaments that sweep up from front and back of the gondola and add so much to its mysterious profile. Il *fèro da próva*, at the front, serves as a fourteen-kilo counterweight to the gondoliere at the back. Many sources state that the six forward-looking *bròche* (teeth) represent the six sestieri of the two main islands, while the single backward-looking *bròca* stands for la Giudecca, which is geographically separated from the others. The arched neck of the fèrro is said to be the image of the Rialto Bridge, though its equal resemblance to the peculiar cap or *corno* worn by the Doge of Venice is sometimes offered as an explanation.

Corso Delle Cortegiane
In Rio Della Sensa

The *fèro da pòpe*, at the back, is a far less elaborate thing and is there primarily as protection against bumps and scrapes.

Decorated nails placed between the *bròche* do the work of attaching the ferro to the frame of the boat. It is well worth visiting the Museo Correr and the Naval Museum to have a look at their collections of head-spinningly beautiful ferri from gondolas of the last centuries. These examples of the genius of Venetian craftsmen seem, in certain lights, to be made of lace, so delicate is the tracery of figures and arabesques, so light-filled the open spaces. Closer examination reveals their solid fraternity with the carving on the oriel windows on so many Venetian palazzi, where masons worked the same magic with stone and succeeded in making that material appear just as gossamer and weightless as these beaten rods of iron. No wonder the city authorities, after calculating how much time went into creating ferri rather than useful things like spears and cannons, struck back with sumptuary laws that criminalized the iron workers for the production of mere beauty and threatened repeat offenders with eighteen months service in the galleys or three years in prison.

The fórcola, carved from a single piece of walnut root, is the navigational heart of the gondola, for it is in the *mòrso* (opening) that the gondoliere rests his oar while pivoting to make a new stroke. The fórcola must provide different leverage points for the single oar and thus allow the skilled gondoliere to maneuver his gondola through busy canals and narrow waterways.

The evolution of the fórcola can also be studied in the work of the major Venetian painters. It gets shorter, taller, thicker, the second mòrso disappears; it tilts out from the side of the gondola and then moves back closer. The design and carving, however, are on a straight trajectory toward abstract beauty of line and finish. For a time in the nineteenth century, it was painted black, but then taste changed, and it returned to its natural wood finish.

The gondoliere is entirely dependent upon the fórcola to provide a base and pivot for his oar during the countless strokes he makes each day. Only three craftsmen in Venice produce them today, and gondolieri treat them with near-reverence, seeing that they are kept well-rubbed with linseed oil and a home-made paste of Vaseline and oil of Vaseline, a process which will help them last a lifetime. Each one is crafted to a specific gondoliere, with the maestro taking into account his height and weight as he carves the wooden block. One unusual thing about the fórcola is the impossibility of finding anything to compare them to: the fórcola looks like a fórcola, and that's the end of it.

The examples so richly provided by Venetian painters fail to provide accurate information about the last element of the gondola, the oar or *remo*, quite simply because most painters showed them where they spend most of their time: under water. Thus it is difficult to give evidence of how much or little the remo has changed through the centuries. Most are made

of beech and are about 4.2 meters long. The blade tapers and grows both wider and thinner at the end, to facilitate its passage through the water and to increase the power of its thrust.

The gondola, then, is a composite of apparently odd pieces put together with rigorous accuracy, still assembled in the same way as it has been for hundreds of years. The clothing of the people walking on the streets of Venice today looks different from the clothing of those who walked here a half a millennium ago. The articles in the shops of this most commercial of cities are entirely different. Yet the fabric of the city remains the same: the same facades, the same hand-made glass in some windows, the same paving stones. And gliding by, there is the same dark shadow with the single man standing in the back, calling out a soft *"Oii"* to warn of his coming.

The Master Builder

One of the common experiences of too-frequent travel is the phenomenon of waking up in a hotel room with no idea of where the room is: what city, what country, what continent. Experience teaches us to lie still and study the patterns of light, and once the source is discovered, memory of the location usually follows.

To enter into the squero, or boathouse, where the Tramontin family has been building gondolas for four generations is to experience a similar sensation of complete dislocation. This time, however, it is not the dresser in the wrong place that provokes geographic confusion but the objects in the large room which lead to a feeling of complete chronological displacement, for there is nothing to give a sign of year or epoch, nor would it be easy to guess the century. To right and left there are two gondolas raised on wooden cradles. A young man leans over the one on the left, planning away at a wooden board with a hand-held plane identical to one my grandfather used. The boy on the right holds a slim hammer and taps small wooden pegs into the holes in a board that must have been made by the hand-propelled drill that lies at his feet. Luckily, he's wearing one item that provide temporal

orientation: a new pair of red Converse sneakers.

Roberto Tramontin, the *maestro*, steps up and shakes my hand; small bones adjust themselves to more comfortable positions. Tramontin is tall and thick, with the muscled body of a man who works hard all day and likes to eat and drink. His eyes are blue, as are the eyes of many Venetians, and his remaining hair is black. His smile is easy and relaxed, his teeth perfect. He goes back to what he was doing, feeding small pieces of scrap wood into an old metal stove with a tall tin pipe that disappears out of the roof. The stove, which gives an occasional burp of black smoke, manages to warm nothing beyond a half meter from it and leaves the rest of the cement-floored squero cold. And damp.

On the far wall hangs an old black and white photo of his father, who taught him what he knows, though he says it took him 24 years to learn enough to make a gondola on his own. He starts to talk about perfection and the necessity, which he insists is absolute, that this perfection reside in every one of the pieces in a gondola, whether they are visible or invisible. Any imperfection will destroy the whole, he insists, and I see how serious he is about this by the way he keeps an eye on every shaving that peels away from the apprentice's plane.

Only five squeri to build gondolas are left in Venice. When I ask him if this decline will affect him and what he thinks the future holds, he explains that, though he usually builds only a single new gondola each year, visiting groups of tourists also bring in extra money, as does repair work, and thus they manage to go on. He has a long list of gondolieri who are willing to wait at least four years to have a gondola made by Tramontin.

A gondola, he explains, will last on average thirty years, though the bottom part, the *opera viva*, which is constantly under water, needs to be replaced after fifteen, thus providing more work. His eyes move to a large plastic-covered rectangle high on the far wall, and he says, "If I could sell that . . . "

"That," as it turns out, is the Nineteenth Century felze which once formed the central part of the gondola of the Savoia family, the former kings of Italy. It's complete, has five crystal windows, two on each side and the one in front with the Savoia crest burned into it with acid, and the original black

cloth with 32 silk pompons. He restored it completely some years ago, part of which process entailed stripping off layers of paint and gilding. "When they had no money, the Savoias had it painted, and when the money came in, they had it gilded again."

He would like to sell it and offers me 10% of the selling price to advertise it successfully. When I renounce the idea of the 10%, our friendship deepens, and he returns his attention to the two gondolas: the first is to go to an exposition in Munich and then be brought back to be used as a traghetto gondola; the other is for a private client, another gondoliere. Since we'd become, however fleetingly, business partners, I asked if he knew what a gondola license costs.

"The official price is seventy thousand Euros," came his prompt reply.

"*Prezzo ufficiale*," is the Italian equivalent of Santa Claus, so silence was the only suitable response. "Probably ten times that," he offered into my continuing silence. At present, he told me, there are 425 gondola licenses, though the city is about to offer eight more. The owner can use it or sell it or leave it to his son. Or, presumably, to his daughter, but since there is only one woman gondoliere, and she didn't pass the rigorous tests that allow entrance into the guild until 2010, that might not be a wise decision. For what it is worth, rumor has it that a taxi license sells for a million, though Tramontin joined with the two apprentices in thinking this an exaggeration.

I asked him about the tools lined on the walls and used by the apprentices, most of them wooden and hand-made and many of them with their parts joined together by elaborate hemp bindings. He explained that they were used by his great-grandfather, who had opened the squero on 2 February, 1884, also by his grandfather, then paused to add that the grandfather of his great-grandfather had been a gondoliere, as if to ward off any suspicion that this family had insufficient salt water in its veins.

He was taught to make his calculations in the Venetian *piede*, which is divided into twelve *once* for a total of 347.73 mm or 13.69 inches. Tramontin explained that it is far easier for him to remember the lengths of the various pieces in piedi, which are given in whole numbers for the gondola, rather than in meters or centimeters, which demands multiplying numbers that have been carried out to three decimal places. The young apprentices have to adapt to this system: he's too old to change his ways.

The past was never far from us there; he spoke as if a rush order that arrived in 1925 had come in that morning. To fill it, the two men working in the squero, his father and his grandfather, built 7 gondolas in 21 days and even managed to complete one entire boat in the space of 24 hours. Yes, the pieces had already been cut – by hand, please note – but they managed to put it together in a single day. It was obvious that he was as proud of this triumph as if he had taken part in it himself.

He took my arm and drew me close to the gondola on the left and pointed to a piece of wood that the process of building was soon to hide by the addition of the planks of the deck. It was, he explained, his signature, a pattern of different-sized triangles cut into the edges of the board, reminiscent of the brand burned into the hide of cattle. When I asked why the piece of wood was placed upside down, further hiding the Tramontin signature, he said that to do it any other way would be vulgar. What he did not have to say was that any gondoliere, seeing the perfection of the boat, would recognize instantly the hand that had built it.

Can a Boat Be a Fashion Statement?

Venice is a tidal city, a fact evident to anyone who takes a look at the water in the canals. At six-hour intervals, the tide changes direction and either begins to flow out of the *laguna* in which the city rests or to flow in, bringing with it cleaner water from the Adriatic. This natural flow brings shrimp, crabs, and fish into the *bacino* and removes whatever waste has gone into the water since the last tide, a twice-daily cleansing that has happened with predictable exactitude ever since there were tides.

Water is not the only medium that changes in Venice: ever since its foundation, products and fashions have flowed naturally into and out, reaching Venice more quickly than land-locked cities, mountain cities, desert cities. Unlike the tide, which is predictable and measurable, new ideas and new desires slipped in when they will, their force and velocity as impossible to calculate as they are to resist.

The history of Venice contains frequent accounts of the attempts of its rulers to protect the citizens of the city from these other invasive tides, but this has never been an easy thing to achieve. Accustomed as they are to living in a city of twists and turns and *calli* that undulate as if with a will of their own, Venetians were not and are not likely to have any special sympathy for rules or laws that attempt to control the manner in which they are expected to behave. People who see daily evidence of the irresistible force of nature are not likely to be much interested in restraint or the attempt to restrain their desires. City authorities, faced with the invasive tides of luxury goods and adornment, attempted to heap up legal dykes and sea walls to block their entry to the city. The cause of this, I believe, was economic. An English poet wrote, "Getting and spending, we lay waste our powers." This was a truth known only too well by the original guardians of Venice's wealth and well-being (often considered as one and the same). Consider for a moment: money spent on transitory beauty – a dress, a brocade jacket, a new pair of satin shoes – is money that is removed from the solid, accumulated wealth of the city. It is paid to foreign exporters: the silk, the design, the manufacture were likely to come from France or the Orient, so the money escaped from the city and thus would do nothing to further its glory or its power. What is more transitory than a fashionable garment? This year's glory is next year's cleaning rag. A palazzo, a pile of gold ducats: these were examples of real wealth, not some whim of fashion that could evaporate as quickly as it was created. Of course, the prohibitions against outward displays of luxury and extravagance were presented in the costume of morality and religion: a plainly-dressed woman was likely to be a virtuous woman. A Sixteenth Century law declared that

the collars of women's dresses could not bear any hand-worked decoration – *"al collo nessun lavoro."* Could this have been a response to the statistic-gathering city administration's report, which does not mention the nature of the sewing on their collars, of 11,164 prostitutes working within the city in 1509? Five years later, the city formally established and empowered the *Provveditori alle Pompe* to oversee and enforce the sumptuary laws: the number of rings, necklaces, even courses at dinners was to be strictly regulated.

But the wily, beauty-seeking, pleasure-seeking Venetians seemed able – much in the manner of today's athletes, whose performance-enhancing drugs remain one long stride ahead of the blood tests meant to detect yesterday's drugs – to elude the enforcers of the sumptuary laws: why else would more and more detailed laws need to be passed? The prohibition against gold and silver as personal adornment is a common thread in the story of these laws. Trade was based on these two elements, and the authorities would not tolerate their being frittered away in mere decoration, certainly not when there was the entire Orient in which they could be invested and made to grow.

At this point, the question, "Where'd the gondola go?" would be quite in order. It was floating both ahead of and amidst the other conspicuous proofs of Venice's wealth and ability to consume and thus attracting to itself the Basilisk eye of the Provveditoriato alle Pompe, ever ready to interfere when they sensed that someone was spending too much money on the evanescent rather than on the permanent. It was at this time that the decoration of the gondola was severely regulated and the adornment limited to the severe form of the ferro that can still be seen today. The records exist: on 8 October, 1562, the Senate forbade "boats that are not plain" and forbade any felze that was gilded or painted and carved." This apparently didn't work, for by 1584, anyone who dared to row a boat that was too elaborate risked "prison, the galleys" or the very menacing "other."

What did the gondola, taking women and men to meet friends or lovers, contribute to the economic betterment of the city? How was trade advanced by these *laguna*-bound boats, capable of transporting only a few people and then usually at the pace of a walking man?

Centuries before, they had carried the population to safety from the invading hordes from the North, but that had been a passive service, like the taxis that carried troops to the defense of Paris in 1914. What heroic defense of the city was ever made by the gondola? During the Battle of Chioggia in 1380, it was the fleet of war ships and not the puny gondola that won the victory.

The gondola, however, was never intended for defense or attack, only as a means of transportation, and as that it is an unqualified success story. By the 18th century, there were somewhere between eight and ten thousand gondolas.

Venetians used them as a means of easy transportation through their tangled city, and their decks became a common source of musical entertainment. Even then, it should be noted, the gondola was vastly outnumbered by boats serving the commercial interests of the city. A look at the paintings of Guardi and Canaletto suggests a reality as true today as hundreds of years ago: most boats in Venice are not gondolas. People have the option of walking to the Rialto Market. Cabbages do not.

Today, in a world run mad with the idea of image, the stature of the gondola has increased, regardless of its cosmetic changes. Las Vegas wants some, and gondola builders send them all over the world. Many of the foreigners who come to Venice to be married insist that a gondola be part of the ceremony. Miniature plastic gondolas – some lit from within – are on sale in many Venetian shops, as are glass ones. There are eyeglass frames in the shape of a gondola. The silhouette can be seen on T-shirts and coffee mugs, silk scarves and ties. There are gondola ashtrays and ceramic plates and plaques with gondolas. And the gondola hat is known as just that.

During the day, this tourist kitsch is laughable, but it cannot extinguish the fascination. A late-night walker, crossing a bridge or approaching a *riva*, will sometimes sense, not hear, the sibilant approach of a gondola, its prow slipping through the waters. Or perhaps the ferro will emerge from a winter fog for a moment, slide by, only to disappear again, a bit farther on.

The moment lies somewhere between the mysterious and the magical, and perhaps the unsung melody of a barcarola is in the air: it's there and then it's not. It could be happening now, but it could have happened exactly the same way hundreds of years ago in the same way. A tidal city, where things come and go and come again.

Musica Popolare

Opera, though immensely popular with an elite audience in seventeenth and eighteenth century Venice, was an art form aimed at the upper classes. Noblemen and women flocked to the city from all over Europe for the endless revelry of Carnevale and the endless delights of opera. To hear it, the listener had to pay to enter the theater, where professional singers declaimed noble sentiments in the elevated language of poetry. The operas were filled with characters from epics and tragedy: good kings and queens, wicked kings and queens, Tamerlane, Richard the Lionheart, Cleopatra. Yet the dilemmas they faced were unlikely to be confronted by the ordinary citizen in the course of daily life: loss of kingdom, the need to choose between poison or the sword as a means of suicide, the proper handling of a chariot hitched to two fire-breathing dragons.

Ordinary people had quite different ideas about what constituted musical entertainment, and they found it thriving outside of the theaters. They wanted, just as they want today, popular music. Popular. And what could be more popular than the Venetian barcarole, with its origin and its listeners both found among *"la gente del popolo,"* not a music-loving elite. Its origin was *la barca*, the boat, from which it was sung, often by the gondolieri themselves, though sometimes by semi-professional singers accompanied by a small group of musicians.

While the sophisticated arias of opera were performed from the stage of an elaborate theater, and the religious music for which Venice was equally famous was confined to sacred service within a church, the barcarole were simple songs intended to be sung in the open air. What better platform for beauty than the gondola, and what easier way to take the entertainment through the open air from one audience to another? Anyone who happened to be passing by was free to listen to the music and singing without having to attend Mass or pay to enter a theater: it might be history's first example of free download.

The singers were concerned with stories from real life, not with princes, kings, and mythological heroes who, on the opera stage, killed enemies and monsters to rescue the princess. These were simple guys who were interested in the pretty blonde who lived in the house down the *calle*. Instead of conquering the walls of some foreign city, the singer remembered the thrill of going out to the Lido with his pals and girls from the neighborhood like Checca, Betta, and Catte. It's hard to think of anything more popular – or real – than this. The lyrics illustrate daily life in Venice and give voice to the Venetians' eternal desire to make fun of serious things, often contrasting melodies from opera with lyrics as banal as the face of the quite ordinary girl who is the subject of the song. However much his friends tell him she's beautiful, the singer confides to his listeners that this is all a wild exaggeration and she's really quite plain. Instead of a prince who longs for the love of his princess, comparing her to Helen and Venus, we listen to an Armenian transplanted to Venice who can't get his tongue around the local dialect and is reduced to expressing his love for Cattina by singing "Tarapatà *tà tà tà*." Is his love any less real or any less strong for that? There is also an undercurrent of sexuality in some of the lyrics, as in that of the singer who tells his sweetheart that he knows she keeps a garden she has not yet given to anyone. He graciously offers himself as the gardener who would work it for her.

Most of these *canzoni* were anonymous: one did not have to be a famous libretto writer like Metastasio to say that "Many people complain because they don't have enough money in their pocket to pay to have a good time," or "I can't say she's beautiful because she's not beautiful." Another song presents the listeners with a singing teacher whose class is a hilarious failure. These, however, are the songs that people delighted in hearing: even now, centuries later, most Venetians delight at the sound of the first notes of "La biondina in gondoletta" and are happy to sing along.

Consider the location of the performance: on the water, as the gondolas went back and forth, carrying singers, small musical ensembles to accompany them, lovers or wives and husbands, young men in search of adventure, while the people walking by on the embankments, not troubled by false compunction or ideas about proper behavior, shouted back and forth with the singer, called out praise or criticism. *Popolare.*

Not only did this musical world have pre-electric download, it also had copyright infringement. The gondolieri were allowed, by city ordinance, to enter theaters without having to buy a ticket, which meant that they could go into any one of the many opera houses in Venice, listen until they heard a tune

they liked, and then – either by a feat of memory or an act of transcription – go back to work and sing it as they had heard it sung. The original composer, rather than contact his lawyer, was often flattered and helped by this attention, for it would, by immediately disseminating his work to a wider audience, add

to his fame while encouraging some of the public to go to the theater, pay for a ticket, and hear the rest of his opera.

Visitors to the city were apparently as charmed by these songs as were the locals: the Englishman, John Walsh, took the tunes home with him and, in 1742, published a large volume. He was careful, however, to attribute them to well-known composers like Hasse (who does happen to be buried in Venice) and "other celebrated Italian Masters," no doubt to attribute a more respectable provenance to them than to admit that they were the simple products of local musicians, men who sang for the love of it and the sound of it and the fun of it. How terribly popolare, eh?

And what more popolare than the lament of the young woman who discovers that the heart of the man she loves is already full to over flowing? Cecilia Bartoli, special guest artist, unites the world of opera and barcarole and shows the special beauty of both.

The Ships from Hell

Though the gondola is the boat most intimately associated with the city of Venice, many other boats ply the waters of La Serenissima. Some of them – the *sàndolo,* the *caorlìna,* the *peòta* – are propelled, as is the gondola, by oars. Others, the large transport boats that bring in the mineral water and washing machines, have motors, as do the ACTV *vaporetti* that take residents and tourists on long-established routes around the city. All of these boats, even the enormous – at least by normal Venetian standards – vaporetti serve the needs of the residents by moving them around their city and bringing to them the things that are nowadays necessary for the running of their lives. In 2002, the city of Venice reported that public transport made up less than 9% of the water traffic in the historic center of the city. By 2006-7, that number had grown to 13%. During the same years, the transport of merchandise went from 24.5% to 28%.

But. But. But there are now other boats to be seen in the city. Like some of the others, they are propelled by motors: unlike most of the others, they in no way serve the needs of the majority of the citizens of the city. These are the multi-decked cruise ships which – like the ravaging tribes that a thousand years ago drove the inhabitants of the area to flee in terror from their invasion – have come to Venice to endanger the lives of the natives and lay waste the city, though this time they do it with music playing from their decks.

In the face of the original invasion of the Huns and Lombards, brave Venetian leaders led their fellows to seek shelter from the approaching enemy in the marshes not far from the mainland and subsequently radiated out from the city they built in the midst of the pristine waters of the *laguna* to fight their way to the creation of an empire. The men who rule the city today, however, demonstrate significantly less far-sightedness in the face of an insidious invasion which puts the city at risk.

Caesar tells us that all Gaul is divided into three parts. Common sense tells us that all Venice is divided into two: those who are in favor of the cruise ships and those who hate them. In favor are those who stand to profit from the arrival of an extra few million tourists each year: everyone else in the city falls into the second category.

Those who argue in favor of continuing to permit the boats to block out the sight of the Basilica di San Marco from the other side of the canal, to pollute the air with their engines (about which more in a moment) to create waves that eat at the foundations of the buildings – in short, to hasten the destruction of the city and its residents – can present only financial profit as a motive. One recalls the famous remark attributed to an

American officer during the Vietnam War: "we had to destroy the village in order to save it."

The cruise ships, long a sore in the eyes of most residents, have been slipping in and out of the city for years, though it is only recently, as their effects on the welfare of the city and its residents have become more evident, that the infection been recognized as a full-blown disease. Various groups of citizens who are concerned about the damage caused by the cruise ships have published some numbers and information which non-Venetians might find interesting. Their research has discovered that 405 cruise ships docked in Venice in 2004. By 2010, there were 629, an increase of more than 50% in six years. The ships, however, like so many of their passengers, have grown much bigger, so the total number of passengers in those years went from 677,617 to 1,617,011. In 2011, in the single week of 23-30 July, 77 cruise ships passed in front of San Marco. The largest of these was 311 meters long (that's six Olympic swimming pools, in case you were looking for a way to judge the length) and 48 meters wide. This boat displaced 134,352 cubic meters of water, and if you can figure out how many swimming pools that is, good for you. As any boat moves through the water, the force of its passage displaces the water, which is forced to the sides and, presumably, will bang against the first obstacle it encounters. How much force is exerted by one hundred and thirty-four thousand cubic meters of water, pushed, propelled, shoved aside in a narrow passage lined with embankments and houses on both sides? And what is the effect upon the embankments of the repeated force of that amount of moving water?

Could this explain why the windows of the houses along the embankment shake and why cracks appear in the walls of the buildings? Does this have anything to do with the fact that the embankment of the Giudecca had to be enforced with concrete some years ago? And what about the sediment in this canal, reported in many scientific analyses to be filled with dioxin and heavy metals? How healthy for the people living near that water and the fish that swim in that water (brave survivors that they are, dear little things) to have the propellers of these behemoths stir up the sediment? Here it should be noted that these same canals were the places where many Venetians still living today learned to swim and went fishing. Who would risk that now?

Then there is the fuel burned by these ships. It has been repeatedly cited in *Il Gazzettino,* that journalistic Bible of the city, that the motors of each of these cruise ships, which must keep running 24 hours a day to produce the electricity which the city is not equipped to provide to the port, is the equivalent, in terms of pollution, of having the motors of 14,000 cars left running all day long. On some days there are five of these monsters moored at San Basilio. My math tells me that I now breathe the air of a city where, during much of the year, 70,000 cars are parked, their motors running all day long, a kilometer from my home. More preoccupying, a 2007 study stated that the bunker fuel used by many ships has 2,000 times the sulfur content of the usual diesel fuel used by cars and buses, but I'd prefer not to calculate how many cars that means. Nowhere have I read which type is used by the cruise ships that dock in Venice, though I have read many articles about the breaking of anti-pollution laws by many cruise ship lines. Thus I do not know which burning fuel fills the air with its smell during much of the summer. Tourists used to complain that the stagnant water of the canals created an unpleasant smell during part of the year, yet nowhere was it ever said that the smell was highly toxic, as high-sulfur fumes have been determined to be.

There is little scientific doubt about the correlation between air pollution and lung cancer: the WHO has calculated just how much particulate matter in the air will cause mortality to increase, and by what percentage. Further, they have published a study reporting that, until now, the link between diesel fuel and lung cancer has been underestimated. Even the Chinese are worried, for God's sake. Venetians, however, need not concern themselves with such things because the health service of Venice has not rendered the relevant statistical studies of mortality public since 2002, when it projected numbers of deaths up until 2009. That report, however, suggested that Venice is the Italian city with the highest incidence of lung cancer. Though there is no proof that the cruise ships are the cause, there is no proof that they are not.

Once the ships clear their moorings and move out to the open waters of the Adriatic, they are subject to the muddle of laws regarding what can and cannot be dumped into the waters in which cruise ships sail or burned and let free in the air around them. They are meant to control the dumping of substances such as dry cleaning fluids, paint, solvents, heavy metals, batteries, to make no mention of human waste. Some laws exist, as well, about what can and what cannot be burned, and where, in the incinerators of cruise ships, yet one researcher states that cruise ships incinerate hazardous waste, oil, oily sludge, sewage sludge, medical and bio-hazardous waste, outdated pharmaceuticals, as well as plastics, paper, metal, and glass.

In return for this damage, the 58,000 residents of the city are offered the promise of economic reward: the Port Authority will earn more docking fees, and shops in a city that already suffocates under the presence of millions of tourists will have a few million more. Passengers on cruise ships sleep and can eat on their boats, so hotels and restaurants are unlikely to share in the spoils.

Citizens and residents protest, organize committees, sign petitions, stand at the side of the Canale della Giudecca and hold up signs telling the tourists their cruise ships are not wanted. The local government gives a benign smile, and more and more cruise ships receive permission to sail past, dwarfing the cupolas of the Basilica. One looks out into the Bacino or into the even more narrow waters of the Canale della Giudecca, and the ghost image of the Costa Concordia, still lying like a dead whale in the waters off the Isola del Giglio, flashes into memory, as does the claim of an employee of the White Star Line's Titanic that "not even God himself could sink this ship." The happy tourists on the decks wave back at the friendly natives, and all of those hundreds of thousands of cubic meters of displaced water continue to slide across to the rivas on both sides of the canal to give the city the Kiss of Death.

Barcarole
Venetian – English

Translations by
Shaul Bassi and Philip Morre

Con Checca, Betta e Catte

Con Checca, Betta e Catte
S'avemo devertio
Da la Zuècca à Lio
Senz' esserghe un da dir

Con poco lo sticchemo
Perché regola avemo
E co' sta brava dosa
No se pol mai fallir

With Checca, Betta and Catte

With Catte and Betta and Checca
We had a such a day when we went
To the Lido all the way from Giudecca
That we'd no cause at all to lament

We settle for less than other men do,
For gentle's the grace of the strong,
With a cargo like this to attend to,
Could we ever (oh never!) go wrong?

Madam carissima

Madam carissima
Alla lezion
E franca subito
Vu bien danzè
Datevi animo
Che vi certifico
Che vi certifico
Che riuscirè
Allor con spirito
Madam, levè
Allor con spirito
Madam, levè

Da vù desidero
Che adagio ancor
Il piè sollecito
Pronta girè
Ne sia difficile
Il passo celebre

Il passo celebre
Del balanzè
Allor con spirito
Madam, cupè
Allor con spirito
Madam, cupè
Vù sé l'immagine
Della beltà
Qualità nobile

Vù tutte avè
Però non dubito
Che a st'or benissimo
Che a st'or benissimo
Vù ve portè
Allor con spirito
Madam, saltè
Allor con spirito
Madam, saltè

Oh Sweetest Madam

Oh sweetest madam
Let's to the lesson
I see you'll learn quickly
You dance so neatly
Give it your best one
And I assure you
Oh I assure you
You'll do it prettily

To it then with spirit
Madam, come pirouette
To it then with spirit
Madam, come pirouette

Now are you ready
Even more gently
Up with the feet
Twirl them so neat
It's not so arduous
That justly famous
Balancing feat
Adel und Vornehmheit

To it then with spirit
Madam, that coupé
To it then with spirit
Madam, that coupé

You are the image
The image of beauty
More's your nobility
Than all the peerage
Because there's no doubt
That you are already
Oh you're already
Queen of the rout

To it then with spirit
Madam sauté
To it then with spirit
Madam sauté

Per mi aver

Per mi aver Cattina amor
Mi volevi maridar
Star contento in sena el cuor
Tic e toc sentivi far
Tarapatà tà tà tà
D'allegrezza cuor mi fa
Tarapatà tà tà tà
Che mi quanto innamorà

A Taliana mi marchiar
De papuzza far scapin
Barba zuffa mi tagiar
Vestir tutto paregin
Tarapatà tà tà tà ecc
D'allegrezza cuor mi fa
Tarapatà tà tà tà
Che mi quanto innamorà

O Yes, Cattina

Oh yes, Cattina loves me
She wants to marry her man
So we'll be close as kippers
Hear my heart's bim–bam
Tarapatà tà tà tà
It's full right to the brim
Tarapatà tà tà tà
So full of love I am

To Italy I'll go
Make babooshes into slippers
I'll trim my locks and whiskers
Dress like a Paris beau
Tarapatà tà tà tà
It's full right to the brim
Tarapatà tà tà tà
So full of love I am

Cara la mia Ninetta

Cara la mia Ninetta
So che ti ga un zardin
Che no' ti l'à fittà
Se ti me vol son quà
Se ti me vol son quà
Per lavorarlo

Mi son un zardinier
Che sè far el mestier
Per ti el farò di cuor
So quel che parlo

My Darling Ninetta

My darling Ninetta
I know you have a garden
And you haven't let it
When you want me I'm here
When you need me I'm here

In any weather
You know I'm a gardener
I can delve night and day
For you I'll dig lovingly
I mean what I say

Son stuffo morto

Son stuffo morto
De far più chiassi
Co' amici in orto
Spesso a ballar

Con più puttazze tutta la notte
Che le ragazze fà nascer botte
Che'l morbin presto ne fà passar

I'm Sick to the Teeth

Oh, I'm sick to death
To be making merry still
With the lads on the heath
Dancing through to morning

Changing girls and changing
For girls they make ill-will
That spoils the joy of funning

Tanti dise

Tanti dise o cò l'è bela
Una puta che cognosso
Dirghe bella mi no posso
Perché bella no la xe

Se i contasse che l'è bona
O qua sì che no' i minchiona
Ma una cossa per un'altra
Lodar mai razon no ghe

No xe questa la contesa
Né in chiettini me n'intrigo
Mi sostento nome e digo
Che bel muso no la ga

L'ha do occhi gattesini
E ch'è troppo pizzenini
Un nasetto rebeccao
Tutto el fronte xe rappà

Though Many Say

Though many say she's lovely
That's not what meets my eye
I know her like a brother

And lovely? No, say I.
Were they to say she's saintly
They wouldn't tell a lie
But one thing's not the other:
Calling lamb what's mutton

Just can't be right or sane
I'm not one for perjury
I'm careful of my name
I say her face is plain

Her eyes are like a kitten's
As tiny as two buttons
Her nose a pekinese's
Her forehead full of creases

Mai se patisce freddo

Mai se patisce freddo
Co' donne se ga appresso
Già un gran calor quel sesso
Da qual se sia staggion

Perché mi son giazzà
Le voggio sempre arente
Le xe de mi contente
Perché no' son baron

You'll never feel cold at night

You'll never feel cold at night
With a woman to hold you tight
The fairest keep you from freezing
They boil whatever the season

When I'm frozen as a bear
I keep one always near
I'm as happy to be me
As an honest man can be

La luna mi ghò suso

La luna mi ghò suso
Nò sò quel che me fazza
Una certa ragazza
Xe causa de sto mal

La fa de mi gramazzo
Bordello e gran strapazzo
Come che fusse un storno
O qualche carnoval

I'm Glum As the Moon

I'm glum as the moon
I don't know how she's doing it
That girl that drives me mad
It's because she puts me through it

that I've gone to the bad
I rampage rudderless
as a riot of revelers
or a one man carnival

Confesso el vero

Confesso el vero
Caro musotto
Par vù son cotto
Che gnanca che

Ma se credessi
Occhi tiranni
De darme affanni
Vù la fallè
De darme affanni
Vù la fallè
Si si mie viscere
Vù la fallè

V'ho ditto è vero
Che v'amo e adoro
Che'l mio tesoro
Vù sé, e'l mio ben.

Ma co ste dura
No ghe più caso
La mosca al naso
Presto me vien
Si si mie viscere
Presto me vien
Si si mie viscere
Presto me vien

I Must Confess

I must confess
Dear little morsel
I'm lost, I'm quite lost for you
And no one more so

But if you go thinking
With your tyrannous eyes
You can make me helpless
You are mistaken
You can make me helpless
You are mistaken
Yes, yes my paradise
You are mistaken

I'm not telling lies
I love you and adore you
My treasure is all of you
and my good besides

But if you play the hard one
I'll soon change my mind
an assault on my blindside
soon twists my bacon
yes yes my paradise
soon twists my bacon
yes yes my paradise
soon twists my bacon

Molti rogna

Molti rogna perché in berta
No'i gha bezzi da far chiasso
El' so cuor per cossa certa
Da passion ghe va in sconquasso
El' so cuor per cossa certa
Da passion ghe va in sconquasso

I fà pecà gramazzi
A vederli a smaniar
Per no poder far sguazzi
Come i soleva far

So Many Men Complain

So many men complain
of holes in their purses
No coin for excursions
That their hearts for the strain
Go to pieces
The rage drives them witless

They're pitiful to witness
rampaging around
Having no money
To throw on the ground

Farev' la ritrosetta

Farev' la ritrosetta
Senza un fià de pietà
La mia gran fedeltà
Ve mova a compassion

Sto gran mio cuor aspetta
E sempre afflitto son
Ve mova via caretta
La mia crudel passion

You Play the Shy One

You play the shy one
With never an ounce of pity
Doesn't my loyalty
Nudge your compassion?

My great heart is waiting,
Unending my affliction.
When will I move you, my darling,
My cruelty, my passion?

La biondina in gondoletta

La biondina in gondoletta
L'altra sera ghò menà
Dal piacer la poveretta
Là s'à in botta indormenzà

La dormiva in su sto brazzo
Ogni tanto la svegiava,
Ma la barca che ninava
La tornava a indormenzar

The Blonde in a Gondola

I went rowing the other night
with my blonde in a gondola:
Poor thing, such was her delight
That she fell asleep instantly

And in my arms she nestled
I woke her from time to time,
but the rocking of our vessel
soon sent her back to dreaming.

Se imparar la vuol patrona

Se imparar la vuol patrona
Ben de musica a cantar
Sto contento la me dona
La me ascolti a solfeggiar
Do, re, mi, fa, sol
La me ascolti a solfeggiar

Che gran aria galantina
Che maniera che parlar
Una bona cantarina
Ella gà a diventar
Do, re, mi, fa, sol
La me ascolti a solfeggiar

Del teatro tanto pien
No se ghe poder star
Perchè ella tanto ben
Lesta saverà incontrar
Do, re, mi, fa, sol
La me ascolti a solfeggiar

Alle stelle voi che arriva
Coi palchetti zo buttar
E più strepito xe i viva
E i sonetti e solfeggiar
Do, re, mi, fa, sol
La me ascolti a solfeggiar

You Want to Learn My Lady

You want to learn my lady
How to sing beautifully?
I'm happy to teach you
Here's my solfeggio
do, re, mi, fa, sol, la, ti, do
There's my solfeggio

What poise we shall see
What impeccable diction
What a perfect tune
What marvellous poetry
do, re, mi, fa, sol, la, ti, do
There's my solfeggio

The theater will be bursting
Not one place unsold
Your lovely song soaring
To conquer the world
do, re, mi, fa, sol, la, ti, do
There's my solfeggio

How your voice rises
Hear the boxes roar
You reach for the skies
To Encore and Encore
do, re, mi, fa, sol, la, ti, do
There's my solfeggio

Mi credeva d'esser sola

Mi credeva d'esser sola
Ma ti ga cento morose
Va pur là, che ste smorfiose
Tute quante goderà

Za lo so che le ga stizza
Perché qua ti è pronto e lesto
Va, consolile pur presto
Cossì tuto finirà

A sta sorte de putazze
Salvarla farghela bela
Se le crede, no so quela
Che me vogia afani tior

Se a la prima lo saveva
No tirava tanto avanti
Perché el tendarghe a birbanti
De una puta non è l'onor

Vago in leto che so straca
Stufa so de far parole
Va da quele banderiole
che ti è muso d'andar là

Se m'ò perso in ti più mesi
Non ti pol taserme un fiao
Se ti avessi mormorao
Certo un di la pairà

I Thought I Was the Only One

I thought I was the only one
Now I hear there's a hundred others
Run after your simpering lovers
Pay court to the whole ton
I know they're all sore about you
You're in a such a tearing hurry
Run, tell them not to worry
We'll manage here without you

Surely baggages like that
Merit everything you've got
You believe that? Then I wonder what
can be holding you back
If only I'd known earlier
I wouldn't have been so willing
Giving herself to a villain
Is no honour to a girl

Well, I'll be off to my bed
I'm tired of too much talking
If you like to hear doxies' squawking
You know where to lay your head
They were wasted days I admit it
I loved you and couldn't hold you
Don't say I never told you
One of these days you'll regret it

Music Credits

The eighteenth-century barcarole listed can be heard on the enclosed CD, along with the following chamber music interludes:

Al prato e al cale o ninfe
instrumental version
violin, archlute, theorbo

Con Checca, Betta e Catte
3 violins, baroque guitar, theorbo, cello, harpsichord

Madam carissima
2 violins, viola, cello, theorbo, archlute, harpsichord

Per mi aver
cornetto, cello, baroque guitar

Cara la mia Ninetta
viola d'amore, archlute, cello

Domenico Gallo (1730 – 1768 ca.)
Trio sonata No. 1 in G major
Moderato – Andantino – Presto
2 violins, cello, theorbo, harpsichord

Son stuffo morto
harpsichord

Tanti dise
violin, baroque guitar, archlute, cello, harpsichord,

Mai se patisce freddo
2 violins "in tromba marina", cello, baroque guitar, milanese
mandolin, harpsichord

La luna mi ghò suso
oboe, cello, harpsichord

Pietro Baldassare (1683 ca. – 1768 ca.)
Sonate for cornet, strings and continuo in F maj.
Allegro – Grave – Allegro

Confesso el vero
Neapolitanische Mandoline, Mailänder Mandoline, Violine,
archlute, Cembalo

Giuseppe Tartini (1692 – 1770)
Canzone veneziana
from: Sonate No. XII in G major for solo violin
solo violin

Molti rogna
2 violins, cello, archlute, theorbo, harpsichord

Farev' la ritrosetta
2 violins, baroque guitar, archlute, cello, harpsichord

Giuseppe Antonio Brescianello (1690 ca. – 1758)
Trio Sonata in c minor for violin, oboe and continuo
Largo – Allegro – Adagio – Allegro
oboe, violin, cello, archlute, theorbo, harpsichord

La biondina in gondoletta
romantic guitar

Se imparar la vuol patrona
cornetto, violin "in tromba marina", violin, cello,
milanese mandolin, baroque guitar, archlute, harpsichord,

Bonus track with Cecilia Bartoli: ***Mi credeva d'esser sola***
violin, archlute

Il Pomo d'Oro: Cast

Riccardo Minasi	violin, violin "in tromba marina", viola d'amore, direction
Boris Begelman	violin, violin "in tromba marina"
Giulio D'Alessio	violin, viola, neapolitan mandolin
Ludovico Minasi	cello
Patrick Beaugiraud	oboe
Maxim Emelyanychev	harpsichord, cornetto
Simone Vallerotonda	archlute, theorbo, baroque guitar
Ivano Zanenghi	archlute, milanese mandolin, romantic guitar
Riccardo Coelati-Rama	doublebass
Andrea Perugi	harpsichord (Pietro Baldassare)
Vincenzo Capezzuto	singer

With heartfelt thanks to **Cecilia Bartoli** *for the bonus track*

Recording: Jean-Daniel Noir, Villa San Fermo, Lonigo, May 2012

Executive Producers: Gesine Lübben, Giulio D'Alessio

All of the recordings on the enclosed CD were made specifically for this project by Vincenzo Capezzuto *Il Pomo d'Oro*. All arrangements by: Riccardo Minasi

With heartfelt thanks from Vincenzo Capezzuto to Claudio Borgianni, Cristina Calzolari, and Bruno Moretti

Donna Leon

Donna Leon was born in New Jersey in 1942, but she has lived in Venice since 1981. Commissario Guido Brunetti brought Leon international fame, but baroque music is no less important to her. In 2011, she was named the honorary president of the Venetian Centre for Baroque Music, which is devoted to the promotion and dissemination of baroque music in all its many forms. She has written two previous books accompanied by CDs, *Handel's Bestiary* and *Venetian Curiosities*.

Il Pomo d'Oro

Founded in 2012, the chamber orchestra Il Pomo d'Oro has made a name for itself within a short time with its award-winning recordings of baroque music played on original instruments. Their first CD, under the direction of violinist Riccardo Minasi, was a recording of *L'Imperatore* by Antonio Vivaldi. Their latest CD is dedicated to the quintessential Venetian song, the bacarole.

Illustration Credits

2 Canaletto (Giovanni Antonio Canal): 'The Mouth of the Grand Canal looking West towards the Carità', c. 1729/30 (detail)
The Royal Collection. Photo: Copyright © 2011 Her Majesty Queen Elizabeth II/The Bridgeman Art Library

6 + 49 Giovanni di Niccolò Mansueti: 'The Miraculous Healing of the Daughter of Begnvenudo', c. 1502 (p. 6 detail)
Galleria dell' Academia, Venice. Photo: Copyright © Cameraphoto Arte Venezia/The Bridgeman Art Library

8 Canaletto (Giovanni Antonio Canal): 'Saint Mark's Square towards South and West', 1739/40 (detail)
Courtesy of Derek Johns Ltd., London

10/11 Gentile Bellini: 'Miracle of the Cross at the Bridge of San Lorenzo', c. 1500
Courtesy of the Ministero Beni e Att. Culturali. Photo: Copyright © Scala, Florenz

16 + 19 Gondola Construction plan Plate 1 by Gilberto Penzo, 1993 (p. 16: the stern. p. 19: the prow)
'Rilievi, piani di costruzione, modelli di barche adriatiche'. Copyright © 1993 Gilberto Penzo, Venice

20/21   Canaletto (Giovanni Antonio Canal): 'The Bacino di San
               Marco on Ascencion Day', c. 1733/34
+ 64   The Royal Collection. Photo: Copyright © 2011 Her
               Majesty Queen Elizabeth II/The Bridgeman Art Library
               (p. 64 details)

23   Canaletto (Giovanni Antonio Canal): 'A Regatta on the
               Grand Canal', c. 1740 (detail)
               National Gallery, London. Photo: Copyright © The
               Bridgeman Art Library

26/27   Canaletto (Giovanni Antonio Canal): 'View of Piazzetta
               of Bacino di San Marco with Libreria, Torre del Orologio
               and Basilica di San Marco'. Section from painting 'The
               Doge Palace', 1750
               Galleria degli Uffizi, Florence. Photo: Copyright © akg-
               images/Rabatti – Domingie

31   Canaletto (Giovanni Antonio Canal): 'Regatta on the
               Grand Canal from Ca' Foscari', c. 1740 (detail)
               Windsor, Royal Borough Museum Collection. Photo:
               Copyright © 2013 DeAgostini Picture Library/Scala,
               Florence

32/33   Canaletto (Giovanni Antonio Canal): 'The Grand Canal
               from the Campo San Vio, Venice, about 1728
               Copyright © Scottish National Galleries, Edinburgh

36   Vittore Carpaccio: 'Hunting on the Lagoon', about
               1490–1495, Oil on panel, unframed 75.6 x 63.8 cm (29 ¾ x
               25 1/8 in.)
               Copyright © The J. Paul Getty Museum, Los Angeles

38/39   Gabriele Bella: 'The Women's Regatta on the Grand
         Canal, Venice', ante 1782 (?)
         Galleria Querini-Stampalia, Venice. Photo: Copyright ©
         The Bridgeman Art Library

40   Canaletto (Giovanni Antonio Canal): 'The Customs
         House and the Riva della Zattera', undated (detail)
         Milan, Crespi Collection. Photo: Copyright © 2013 Scala,
         Florence

43 + 46 Canaletto (Giovanni Antonio Canal): 'Reception of the
         Imperial Ambassador at the Doge's Palace', 1729 (details)
         Milan, Crespi Collection. Photo: Copyright © 2013 Scala,
         Florence

44/45   Michele Marieschi: 'Veduta of the Palazzo Ducale at the
         Bacino di San Marco against Santa Maria Della Salute',
         undated
         Private Collection. Photo: Copyright © Artothek

50   Canaletto (Giovanni Antonio Canal): 'River of the
         Beggars', 1723/24 (detail)
         Ca' Rezzonico, Museo del Settecento, Venice. Photo:
         Copyright © Alinari/The Bridgeman Art Library

52/53   Gabriele Bella: 'Il Corso delle Cortigiane in Rio della
         Sensa, Venice', post 1779? – ante 1792
         Fondazione Querini Stampalia, Venice. Photo: Copyright
         © Cameraphoto Arte Venezia/The Bridgeman Art Library

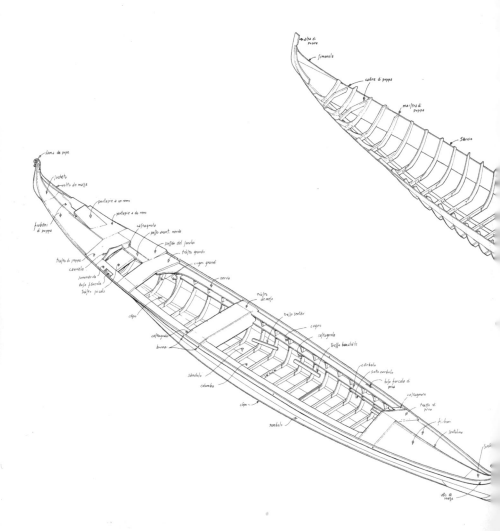

alta di
poppa

timonela

caène di poppa

maistra di
poppa

sàrxio

lama da popa

l'ocheto

volto de mojja

pontapie a un remo

pontapie a do rem

castagnola

pesso avant. nervio

Vessan del fondai

tràfeto grando

cugni grandi

nervio

tràfeto
de mejo

trasto forcler

cugni

castagnola

tràsso banchéte

càrdolo

sota càrdolo

bulo forcola di
pria

castagnola

tràsso di
prùa

fïsubóni
di poppa

tràfeto di poppa

caentela

soenarìa

bulo forcola

tràfeto picolo

cópa

castagnola

bronxi

sàndolo

colómba

cópa

tombolo

fïubóni

fentolino

vali

volto di
mojja